ANIMAL OLYMPIANS

Sporting Champions of the Animal World

David Taylor

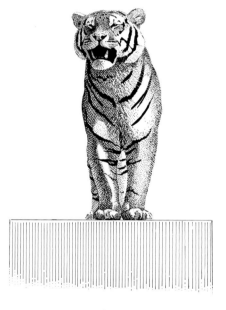

Lerner Publications Company
Minneapolis

All words printed in **bold** are explained in the glossary on page 46.

Front cover: South American spider monkey

First published in the U.S. in 1989 by Lerner Publications Company.

Copyright © 1988 by David Taylor.
Original edition published 1988 by Boxtree, Ltd. London, England under the title DAVID TAYLOR'S ANIMAL OLYMPICS: THE SPORTING CHAMPIONS OF THE ANIMAL WORLD.

Library of Congress Cataloging-in-Publication Data

Taylor, David, 1934-
     Animal olympians: sporting champions of the animal world/David Taylor.
        p.   cm.
     Originally published as: David Taylor's animal olympics. London: Boxtree, 1988.
     Includes index.
     Summary: Compares different kinds of animals regarding their prowess in such categories as jumping, swimming, weight-lifting, and acrobatic movement.
     ISBN 0-8225-2177-6 (lib. bdg.)
     1. Animals—Miscellanea—Juvenile literature. [1. Animals.]
I. Title.
QL49.T22 1989
591—dc19   88-36776
                                                      CIP
                                                       AC

Manufactured in the United States of America

1 2 3 4 5 6 7 8 9 10 98 97 96 95 94 93 92 91 90 89

Contents

Introduction

Many animals are astounding athletes. Among over two million animal species living on earth, we find strong, fast, agile, and graceful creatures—masters of movement in air, on land, and in water.

The Olympic Games are a strictly human affair (although horses are indispensable in the equestrian events). Other animals don't gather in cities such as Seoul and Barcelona every four years to compete in feats of physical excellence. But suppose they did? Just imagine—great though they are—Florence Griffith Joyner, Carl Lewis, Janet Evans, and Greg Louganis would be up against even greater runners, jumpers, swimmers, and divers of the animal kingdom. Not just the large and powerful, but also some of the planet's smallest creatures would compete.

Imagine then, an *Animalympics*. It would have to be held in an open-air stadium, much bigger than any arena built for the human Olympics. Accommodation for the athletes would vary from a little hole in the ground for the ants to an enormous pool for the whales and dolphins. Feeding the competitors would be a major headache. Fresh nectar would have to be brought in daily for the hummingbirds, and the great whales would each need almost 3 tons of krill (small animals resembling shrimp) for their breakfast.

The judges would have the last word sorting out disputes between species, trying to stop killer whales from attacking dolphins in the pool, and preventing tiny insects from getting hopelessly lost among the bigger animal athletes. Lots of records would be broken and much fun had by all. And nobody would miss the only animals not invited—those not-very-talented primates called humans.

Take your seats in the packed stadium. Light the torch. On with the games!

Sprinting

The Animalympic sprinting competition would attract competitors from all over the animal kingdom. The British *roe deer*, with a maximum recorded speed of 38 miles per hour (64 kilometers per hour), and the *red deer*, which is capable of 40 miles per hour (67 kph) would both make a strong showing in the quarterfinals. By comparison, *racehorses* have been known to reach just over 41 miles per hour (69 kph), while human athletic champions have strained to cover 110 yards (100 meters) at just 29 miles per hour (48 kph).

The *caracal* or *desert lynx* from the arid lands of the Middle East, Africa, and Asia would make the sprinting semifinals. The elegant caracal (its name comes from the Turkish word meaning "black ear") measures less than 2 feet (60 centimeters) tall at the shoulder and weighs around 35 pounds (16 kilograms). Despite its size, the caracal is almost as fast as another sprinting semifinalist—the cheetah. It is also a good jumper, sometimes leaping into the air to knock down low-flying birds. It is quick enough to kill up to a dozen pigeons feeding on the ground before the rest of the flock can take flight.

Sharp-sighted Hunters

Another semifinalist in the sprinting event would be a kind of hunting dog known as a "sight hound." Humans first **domesticated** the dog over 10,000 years ago. As time passed, different breeds of dog emerged and each breed had different abilities. The first hunting dogs were bred in the Middle East. These were sleek, long-legged animals with long, flexible trunks (bodies). Hunters selected them to pursue game such as gazelles in open desert country. In the chase, sight hounds, or "gazehounds," of this kind relied more on their good eyesight than on their sense of smell. Their descendants include such breeds as the *Afghan*, the *saluki*, and the *greyhound*.

The greyhound is the fastest of all dogs. It has attained speeds of 39 miles per hour (65 kph). The saluki, although not as fast over short distances, has much more stamina than

The caracal is small but speedy.

The saluki is not as fast as the greyhound in the sprint, but it would outstrip the greyhound over several miles.

the greyhound. The saluki is still used by Bedouin (Arab nomads) to hunt gazelles in the desert. It probably cannot exceed 38 miles per hour (64 kph) in the sprint, but it would certainly outrun the greyhound over 2.5 or 3 miles (4 or 5 km). The Afghan hound can reach speeds of only about 29 miles per hour (48 kph).

The Cheetah in Action

The *cheetah* from Africa and Asia is a sprinter that cannot be beaten by any animal. This handsome beast can run at speeds of up to 62 miles per hour (104 kph) over level ground, and dashes of 88 miles per hour (147 kph) have been claimed! Normally, when hunting, the cheetah bounds along at 38 to 48 miles per hour (64 to 80 kph). Unless it can catch its prey within a few hundred yards, however, the cheetah tends to run out of breath. It frequently attacks antelopes. Although somewhat slower than the cheetah, the antelope can keep up its speed for much longer distances. Unlike other cats, the cheetah has claws that remain unsheathed (uncovered) when the animal runs. The claws provide traction and help the cheetah avoid skidding when it pursues its prey.

The cheetah is built for hunting at short distances and high speeds. Unlike the tiger,

When pursuing its prey at full gallop, the cheetah springs forward with both its hind and its fore legs.

Unsheathed claws provide traction and keep the cheetah from skidding when it pursues its prey.

it doesn't specialize in stalking and ambush. A long, flexible backbone and long legs give the cheetah great leverage. Its power comes from strong muscles in its thighs, back, and shoulders. When galloping, the cheetah pushes itself along by arching its back and springing with *both* hind (back) and fore (front) legs. The sequence of movements in a cheetah galloping at full speed is as follows:

1 The hind legs thrust against the ground.
2 The cheetah floats through the air, feet off the ground, legs extended fore and aft.
3 The forefeet land.
4 The hind end comes forward. The back arches.
5 The forefeet dig in and pull the body forward.
6 The cheetah floats through the air again, but this time its back is arched and its hind and fore legs are tucked in.
7 The hind legs land.
8 The back unrolls and the cheetah begins to stretch out.

A female cheetah with her cubs. Ancient peoples used cheetahs to hunt deer and hares. Curiously, adult cheetahs were more easily trained than were cubs.

As the cheetah gains speed, each complete sequence of movements covers a greater distance over the ground. When galloping at 29 miles per hour (48 kph), the cheetah covers about 13 feet (4 m) with each sequence. At 54 miles per hour (90 kph), it covers over 23 feet (7 m).

Cheetahs are easily tamed and were first used for hunting over 3,500 years ago. Medieval European rulers used these "hunting leopards" to run down deer and hares. Cheetahs captured as adults were found to be better hunters and, curiously, were more easily trained than those raised from cubs.

In 1964, a human athlete, Seraphino Antao, raced a cheetah called Habash over 100 yards (91 m) in Kenya. Although Mr. Antao was in the lead at the halfway mark, the cheetah caught him at the tape to win the race by a fraction of a second, in 9.1 seconds!

It wouldn't be difficult for the judges to name the winner in the Animalympic sprinting event. The cheetah would easily take the gold medal. No animal can equal the cheetah's great speed in the sprint.

Jumping

In the jumping competition of our Animalympics, animals of all kinds and sizes would come from every part of the world to compete. The *German shepherd*, which often demonstrates its athletic abilities at dog shows, is a talented jumper. In 1979 two German shepherds scaled an 11.5-foot (3.5-m) wall to set the canine high jump record at the Royal Air Force Police Working Dog Trials in Nottingham, England. Both dogs used their paws to help them scramble over the top of the wall, however. The German shepherd would probably be eliminated in the Animalympic jumping quarterfinals. The *jumping spider* is also a tremendous jumper. Although it measures less than ½ inch (13 mm) in length, the jumping spider can leap on its prey from a distance of more than 4 inches (10 cm). Like other spiders, the jumping spider has no muscles for straightening its legs. But from slow motion photographs we can see that as the jumping spider leaps, it pushes off by rapidly extending the hind pair of its eight legs. How does it do it? It uses **hydraulics**. The spider pumps blood at great speed into its bent legs. The legs immediately extend and launch the spider forward. Despite its athletic talent, the jumping spider would probably be outclassed in the Animalympics by several other great jumpers.

Leaps and Bounds

In the semifinals of our jumping event we would watch the grasshopper, the flea, the bush baby, the kangaroo, the frog, and the click beetle battle it out in a thrilling contest. With their long and muscular hind legs, all frogs are competent jumpers. But the champion is the South African *sharp-nosed frog*, which can cover over 15 feet (4.5 m) in

A powerful jumper, the frog takes to the air.

at a rate of 8 feet (2.4 m) per second and can reach heights of 12 inches (30 cm) in a jump. The flip is *not* the result of a kick of the beetle's legs. The energy for the jump is actually provided by powerful muscles within the beetle's thorax (chest). These muscles contract and in so doing become tense and full of energy. As the muscles contract, the front and back parts of the thorax lock together. When the tension becomes great enough, the two halves finally slip free of one another. This rapid release of pent-up energy throws the insect into the air.

The Australian entrant in the jumping event would naturally be the *kangaroo*. There are 60-odd species of kangaroo and wallaby found in Australia, New Guinea, and nearby islands. The kangaroo, the biggest of all **marsupials**, can bound along for short distances at speeds of up to 37 miles per hour (61 kph). Kangaroos do not normally jump very high—5 feet (1.5 m) is about the limit. But there have been cases of frightened kangaroos, pursued by dogs, clearing 10-foot (3-m) fences. Kangaroos are superb long jumpers, however, with bounds of around 43 feet (13 m) on record. The animal can do this not only because of its long, powerful hind legs, but, more importantly, because it gets energy for each hop from the long, elastic Achilles tendons of its ankles.

The click beetle in mid-jump. The jump can take the insect 12 inches into the air. Power for the jump comes from strong muscles in the beetle's chest.

a single leap. Leaping Lena, a sharp-nosed frog that competed in the "Frog Olympics" in Cape Town, South Africa, in 1954, cleared a remarkable 32.5 feet (9.8 m) in three consecutive leaps.

Another jumping contestant, the *click beetle*, comes from the garden. Over 300 species of this beetle live in the United States and Canada. Its **larvae** are serious pests called *wireworms*, which can destroy plants and crops. The click beetle's name refers to its curious habit of flipping itself out of danger with a loud click. The beetle springs into the air, often somersaulting five or six times before landing. If it lands upside-down, it clicks again and again until it lands right-side-up. The click beetle can travel upwards

An Animalympic jumping competitor on the move

11

The lesser bush baby is the champion of the standing jump.

The animal that can achieve the greatest height from a standing jump is the *lesser bush baby*. This charming little **primate** from Africa weighs only around 9 ounces (250 grams) and measures less than 1 foot (30 cm) in length. Yet it has been seen to jump 7.5 feet (2.25 m) from a standing jump. What explains the spectacular leaping ability of this tiny animal? The bush baby's strong hind limbs are ideally suited for leaping from tree to tree, and the animal's long tail helps provide balance during a jump. Muscles used for jumping make up 10 percent of the bush baby's body weight. This is *double* the percentage of similar muscles found in the human body. It may look like a cuddly ball of fur, but the bush baby is in fact quite an athlete!

Dizzying Heights

As good as they are, the kangaroos and bush babies can't compete with the jumping abilities of some of the insect contestants. The *grasshopper* can make jumps 50 times the length of its body. But it is surpassed by the *flea*, which often jumps **vertically** 130 times its own height! If a human could do that, he or she could easily leap over a block of office buildings or the Eiffel Tower in

When the tiny flea jumps, it accelerates at 20 times the rate at which a Moon rocket leaves the Earth.

To equal the flea's best jump—130 times its own height—a human jumper would have to clear the Eiffel Tower.

Paris. When it takes off, the flea **accelerates** at 20 times the rate at which a Moon rocket escapes from the Earth's atmosphere. It needs immense power to do this—more power than could be provided by the fastest-contracting muscles. What is the flea's secret? The answer lies in a piece of elastic material called *resilin* at the base of the flea's hind legs. When compressed, the resilin stores energy in the same way that a spring stores energy when it is squeezed. Before a jump, the flea compresses the resilin with its slow leg muscles. Then suddenly, the energy is totally discharged and the flea springs upward like a slingshot.

It is clear that sheer distance would not be the determining factor for picking the gold medalist in the Animalympic jumping contest. The judges would have to take into account the size of each animal in relation to the distance it is able to jump. So there is no doubt that the tiny flea would take home the gold!

Swimming

The swimming events would have to be held in an Animalympic-sized pool. The quaint little *Gentoo penguin* would be a popular entrant in the earlier heats. If in danger, this bird can swim almost 24 miles per hour (40 kph). It moves fastest when it is "porpoising"—swimming near the surface and making brief leaps out of the water much like dolphins and porpoises do when they are on the move. All penguins are master swimmers and they are better adapted to an **aquatic** life than any other birds. They waddle comically on land and they cannot fly, but underwater they are swift, graceful, and agile. The penguin's streamlined body is covered by short, shiny feathers that tightly overlap one another. Wings, which are strong, narrow, and as firm as oar blades, provide the bird's power. Its feet do not paddle like those of a duck, but act as rudders, together with the penguin's stubby tail. The cold water of Antarctica does not trouble the penguin, for the bird is **insulated** by its closely packed, waterproof feathers and a layer of blubber (fat) beneath its skin. Blood vessels in the penguin's wings and feet form efficient "radiators." These blood vessels ensure that cold blood returning from the wings and feet is warmed by outgoing blood from the penguin's heart. This system also prevents the penguin from getting frostbite on land.

Marine (seagoing) turtles would surely make it into the swimming semifinals. One might think of these endangered reptiles as steady, slow swimmers. They make great voyages at an average speed of only 4 to 5 miles per hour (6 to 8 kph). But, when alarmed, marine turtles have been known to accelerate up to speeds of 21 miles per

Penguins are better adapted than any other birds to an aquatic life. These Gentoo penguins can reach speeds of 24 miles per hour.

A baby leatherback turtle swims through South African waters.

hour (35 kph). These animals, which are **cold-blooded** like other reptiles, depend on the heat of their surroundings for warmth. Yet marine turtles are often found swimming in cold water. *Leatherback turtles* are excellent swimmers. They can measure over 8 feet (2.4 m) in length, and can weigh as much as 1,500 pounds (675 kg). Leatherbacks live primarily in tropical waters, but may be found as far north as Nova Scotia, Canada. How does a cold-blooded reptile cope with sea temperatures as low as 50°F (10°C)? The answer is that the energy produced by the turtle's muscles when it swims (it does about 40 strokes a minute) raises the leatherback's body temperature. The animal's large body mass also helps it to retain heat.

Another species that would reach the semi-finals is the *squid*—a relative of the octopus and the garden snail. The squid moves through the water by **jet propulsion**. It draws water into its mantle cavity (the mantle is a soft wall that envelops the squid's body organs) and then expels it through a funnel. The force of this discharge propels the squid through the water. Squid are highly mobile and aggressive **carnivores**. Some of the smaller species that live near the surface of the sea can attain speeds of almost 34 miles per hour (56 kph). The so-called *flying squid* is found throughout tropical and temperate seas. It travels fast across the surface of the water in a series of leaps. At times squid have actually landed on the decks of ships. It is quite a shock for a sailor to see such a sea monster come hurtling on deck!

Mammals of the Sea

The *pinnipeds*, aquatic **mammals** including the seals, sea lions, and walruses, would be eliminated from the swimming competition after reaching the semifinals. Seals such as the *gray seal* scull through the water by sweeping their hind flippers from side to

Capable of speeds of over 38 miles per hour, killer whales are some of the fastest animals in the ocean.

side and tucking their fore flippers close to their chests. Sea lions, on the other hand, use their front flippers as powerful oars and their hind flippers assist in steering. The *leopard seal*, which preys on penguins and other creatures, and the *California sea lion* are the fastest of the pinnipeds. Both can reach speeds of 24 miles per hour (40 kph).

The favorites to win the swimming finals would be some of the *cetaceans* (the whales, dolphins, and porpoises). Cetaceans are also mammals and their ancestors once lived on land. Unlike most mammals, cetaceans eventually left the land to live a totally aquatic life. Their bodies gradually **evolved** and became fishlike. They have the streamlined contours of fish. Their front legs have developed into fins and their hind legs have disappeared completely. But, whereas fish are cold-blooded and breathe by means of **gills**, cetaceans are **warm-blooded** and come to the surface to take in air. Great muscles

that run down the cetacean's back provide the animal with its swimming power. These muscles work the animal's horizontal flukes (tail fins), which beat up and down—not from side to side like the tail of a fish. When the flukes move *upward*, they provide the thrust that pushes the animal forward. They do not provide any power when they move back down again. Cetaceans use their fore fins for steering and sometimes for a little bit of paddling when they are moving very slowly. Most dolphin species can travel at up to 24 miles per hour (40 kph). The *common dolphin* can reach speeds of 34 miles per hour (56 kph) when "bow riding"—moving along with the help of the wave created by the bow of a passing ship.

Killer whales, which will prey on anything in the oceans including sharks, bigger whales, and dolphins, can swim at 38 miles per hour (64 kph) and possibly up to 48 miles per hour (80 kph). The killer whale's rounded

forehead helps the animal carve its way through the water. Even big whales can move at great speeds. The *sei whale*, which can weigh 30 tons, can reach a speed of 33 miles per hour (55 kph). The mighty *blue whale* can move its bulk (100 tons or more) at 22 miles per hour (37 kph) for short distances. The animal can maintain 11 to 11.5 miles per hour (18 to 19 kph) virtually nonstop. The pinnipeds and cetaceans are certainly swift, but they are not the fastest creatures in the sea.

Unsurpassed in Speed

Several fish, the *swordfish*, the *bluefin tuna*, and the *sailfish*, would dominate the swimming competition. The swordfish is thought to reach speeds of 55 miles per hour (92 kph) and the bluefin tuna is capable of 63 miles per hour (105 kph). The sailfish, which may reach over 6 feet (18 m) in length, has a known ability to swim at least 65.5 miles per hour (109 kph)! The fish takes its name from its large **dorsal** fin that spreads out like a sail along the animal's back. Sailfish are found all over the world, but are most common in the warm waters off both coasts of North, South, and Central America. For underwater speed that cannot be equaled, the sailfish would certainly win the Animalympic gold medal in swimming.

The sailfish wins the gold, but the killer whale and the squid would also take medals in the Animalympic swimming contest.

Diving

Several marine animals have been found at very great depths of the oceans. But they would not be allowed to enter the Animalympic diving event. A starfish found at 25,027 feet (7,584 m) down in the Mariana Trench of the Pacific Ocean and an octopus spotted at a depth of 26,730 feet (8,100 m) could not compete. Neither could a solelike fish, swimming in permanent darkness 36,006 feet (10,911 m) below the surface, encountered by oceanographer Jacques Piccard in 1960. Yes, these animals do exist in deep waters—along with innumerable little-known and mysterious creatures. But none of them is a *diver*. They live permanently in the abyss without ever seeing sunlight. Were we to bring them up from the ocean depths, they would die. Their bodies could not stand the greatly reduced pressure at the water's surface and some of them would explode! True divers are up breathing air in the sunlight one minute, and far below the next.

Whereas the human Olympics rates divers on the grace and precision of their dives, the Animalympics would judge contestants on the depth and duration of their dives. One competitor to go out in the first heat would be the *great diving beetle*. A fierce carnivore, the beetle dives to catch and eat other aquatic insects, small fish, and tadpoles. Its larvae also hunt prey in the water, using their sickle-shaped jaws to suck the body juices of their victims. The beetle's flattened hind legs function as oars in the water. Although the great diving beetle rarely goes down more than a yard or two (1 or 2 m), it is a fine diver and underwater swimmer.

Fishing Birds Extraordinary

The main contest for the gold in the diving competition would really be fought out between birds and mammals. But one reptile, the *sea turtle*, might make it into the semifinals. The sea turtle can dive 66 feet (20 m) or deeper, but it couldn't match the performance of the *king penguin*. After inhaling deeply, the king penguin can dive at least 875 feet (265 m) and can stay down

The king penguin is at home on the surface of the water or hundreds of feet below.

18

A group of Magellan cormorants. Their arrowlike shape allows them to cut cleanly through the water when they dive.

for about 15 minutes. No diving bird can compare to the king penguin, although the great northern diver (or common loon), the guillemot, and the cormorant would all would do well in the early heats. *Cormorants* are well suited for diving and can reach depths of several hundred feet. Cormorants, like penguins, have more blood vessels and more blood volume for their size than other birds. This enables them to store a lot of oxygen when they dive. Unlike penguins, however, cormorants possess very little insulating fat under the skin. Although this gives them a slim, arrowlike shape—ideal for cutting through the water—they aren't at home in cold surroundings. In Japan and other parts of the world, people have trained cormorants to dive to catch fish. Rings placed around the cormorants' necks prevent the birds from swallowing their prey while they are working.

Look Out Below

As good as birds are at diving, it is the aquatic mammals—the pinnipeds and the cetaceans—that really run away with the honors. The *Weddell seal*, which hunts the dark and icy depths of the Antarctic Ocean for fish and squid, can reach a depth of 1,960 feet (594 m) in a dive that lasts an hour or more. The *California sea lion* can descend to 891 feet (270 m), but must resurface within a few minutes. But in 1988, a giant *elephant seal* rewrote the record books with a dive that measured over 4,000 feet (1,200 m)—a distance equalling the height of three Empire State Buildings stacked on top of each other! Elephant seals routinely make dives of 2,000 feet (600 m) and frequently dive over 60 times per day.

The Weddell seal will stay under the icy Antarctic waters for an hour or more before surfacing.

Freedom of the Deep

How do these animals dive to such depths and then rise rapidly without suffering from the painful disorder called *the bends*, which sometimes afflicts human divers? How do they survive underwater for so long without fresh oxygen? How do they resist the great pressure of the water at such depths? The pinnipeds and cetaceans have several unique features that make these great dives possible.

The bends is caused when nitrogen gas in a diver's body forms bubbles in the blood and tissue. The bubbles can stretch or break body tissue and can impair blood circulation. This condition can be painful and sometimes fatal. The bubbles appear when the diver comes up and the pressure is reduced—just as a bottle of soda pop bubbles when the top is unscrewed and pressure is removed.

One major difference between a seal or sea lion and a person is that the animal does not go below with a large volume of air stored in scuba tanks or supplied by air lines. Underwater, the human diver continuously breathes in fresh air (which is partly nitrogen) from tanks. The nitrogen from this air can dissolve in the diver's blood and tissues and cause the bends.

Most animals, however, can carry only as much air as their lungs will hold during a dive. The seal *empties* its lungs before it dives and carries even less air (and less nitrogen) with it. But the seal still takes down a great deal of oxygen when it dives. The seal possesses two oxygen-storing pigments—hemoglobin in its blood and myoglobin in its muscles—that help it function without fresh air during a long dive. Its heart also beats much more slowly than normal during a dive. This reduces the seal's blood circulation and the use of the precious oxygen.

To prevent its internal organs from being crushed by the pressure of the water, the diving seal closes down spaces that contain large amounts of air. It squeezes its lungs empty, and special blood vessels bulge in its ear and act as a sort of packing material.

Cetaceans have similar adaptations that allow them to dive to great depths without coming to harm. Cetaceans, unlike pinnipeds, descend with *full* lungs. However, as the whale or dolphin dives, it collapses its flexible chest wall, packing its lungs tight and driving air into its windpipe and nasal passages. The animal's windpipe is armored against the pressure by strong bands of heavy gristle. Blood vessels inflate in other empty spaces in the cetacean's body to fill and support them securely. The cetacean takes down extra oxygen in its blood and muscle tissue,

as does the pinniped. It is able to function without fresh oxygen until it surfaces again—an impossibility for human beings.

Bottle-nosed dolphins, which are often seen in amusement parks and aquariums, have been trained to dive to 1,000 feet (300 m). The United States Navy keeps dolphins and pilot whales for various underwater duties during both peace and war, such as locating mines and helping scientists explore the ocean bed.

In the finals of the diving competition we would certainly see the elephant seal, a trained bottle-nosed dolphin, and the king penguin. But one diving contestant would outperform all other competitors. The *sperm whale* will descend 10,000 feet (3,000 m) below the ocean's surface in search of the bottom-dwelling squid on which it loves to dine. This massive whale, which can weigh up to 70 tons, can stay underwater for up to two hours. It sometimes does battle in the chilling darkness far below the waves with the giant squid. Sperm whales can descend and ascend at the incredibly rapid, but apparently safe, rate of 460 to 560 feet (140 to 170 m) per minute. For unmatched diving ability, the sperm whale would certainly take the Animalympic diving gold medal.

The sperm whale takes on the giant squid, 10,000 feet under the sea.

Sailing

The sailing event in the Animalympics might be marred by a series of disqualifications in the early heats. Sailing is the act of moving across the surface of the water using wind as the only source of power. The movement must be controlled, not aimless. Many animals use the wind for extra power as they travel across the water, but they do not actually sail. This is why the duck would have to be struck off the list of sailing competitors. It is true that the duck and similar birds, such as the coot, are often pushed by the wind as they float on the surface of a pond or stream. But this is not their main method of traveling over water. The duck *paddles* with its webbed feet.

The sting of the Portuguese man-of-war is painful, but it will rarely kill a healthy person.

Allowing the duck to compete in the sailing event would be like allowing an Olympic sailor to switch on an auxiliary engine!

Another entrant that would have to be disqualified from the sailing competition is the *pond skater*, a frail-looking insect with long, thin legs. It too is sometimes propelled along by the breeze, but it doesn't truly sail. The pond skater actually *walks* across the water as if it were walking across a glass dance floor. Its feet don't break through the surface of the water, and no part of the insect gets wet.

The *flying fish* would also have to be banned from competition. This tropical fish can shoot out of the water at speeds of up to 38 miles per hour (64 kph), especially when it is pursued by a **predator** fish such as the barracuda. It then takes briefly to the air, assisted in flight by its saillike fin. One flying fish was seen to soar for one and a half minutes, assisted by the wind, before it reentered the water about 1,200 yards (1.1 km) from where it had emerged. Again, this isn't actually sailing. It is the flying fish's tail fin, beating rapidly just before takeoff, that is the fish's principal source of power.

In the end, we would be left with just two contestants in the sailing finals. Both, believe it or not, are jellyfish. One of these, the *Portuguese man-of-war*, is a truly brilliant mariner. The man-of-war's voyages across great oceans are the animal kingdom's equivalent to those of Francis Drake's *Golden Hind* or Thor Heyerdahl's *Kon-Tiki*.

All for One and One for All

The Portuguese man-of-war is a most remarkable animal that looks like a blob of dark blue jelly. It has a pale blue bladder or pouch that is filled with gas. The pouch projects above the surface of the sea and keeps the animal afloat. It also catches the wind and acts as a real sail. The man-of-war isn't actually a true jellyfish. It is a *siphonophore*, a simple, soft-bodied **invertebrate**. Siphonophores have been living in the world's oceans for over 570 million years. When you see a single Portuguese man-of-war, you are actually looking at many animals that are clinging together to form a colony. The individuals that make up the colony are many different shapes and perform many

The Portuguese man-of-war can trim its blue sail and take off with the wind.

23

different functions. Some members of this collective work at feeding and digesting food. Others sense what is going on in the surrounding environment. Some produce the eggs and sperm necessary for reproduction. Others take the form of **tentacles** that can be up to 40 feet (12 m) long and can deliver a powerful sting. Some of the animals are youngsters and some are adults, but they all work together to create a *single* man-of-war.

The sting of the man-of-war can inflict great pain and suffering on the human body and can cause skin rashes, difficulty in breathing, and severe muscle cramps. While the sting of the man-of-war is most alarming, it is rarely fatal to healthy people. Crabs and some birds like to eat beached men-of-war, and do so without ill effect. Turtles that eat them in the open sea suffer little more than temporary irritation of their eyes.

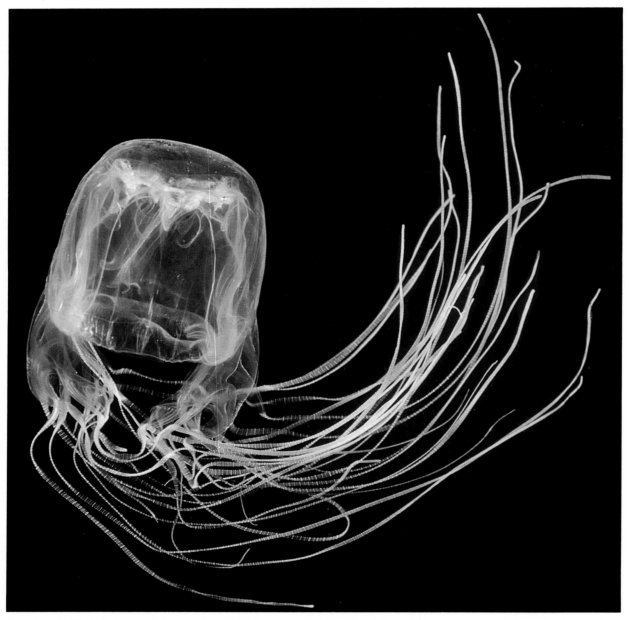

The box jellyfish looks delicate, but its sting can be deadly. The sting is as powerful as the bite of the cobra and can kill a human being.

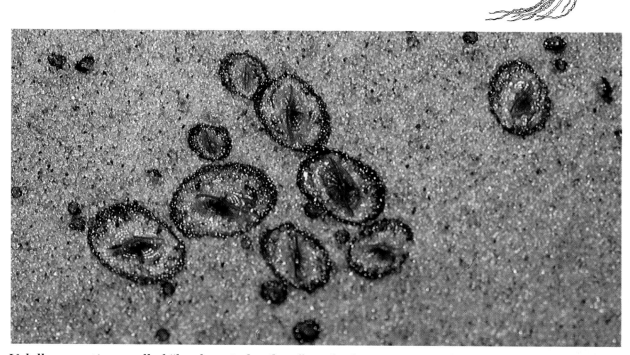

Velella, sometimes called "by-the-wind-sailors," washed up on a Australian beach. The velella travels by the power of the wind, but it can't trim its sail.

Jellyfish to Watch Out For

Much more dangerous jellyfish are the *sea wasps* or *box jellies*, various jellyfish found near the coasts of northern Australia and the Philippines. The sting of one of these creatures is as powerful as the bite of the cobra and can kill a human being. The sea wasp's sting comes from special cells lying on the outer parts of the animal's tentacles. Each of these cells has a hairlike trigger sticking out of it. When a person or animal touches the sea wasp's tentacle, these triggers are set off. Barbed needles spring out from each cell and venom enters the victim through the hollow needles. A person unfortunate enough to come into contact with a stinging jellyfish may have hundreds or even hundreds of thousands of these poison needles enter his or her skin. But the majority of jellyfish are not dangerous. Most people who encounter the animals suffer nothing more than some stinging and redness, which soon disappears. Although the sea wasp is a true jellyfish, it is not a sailor like the Portuguese man-of-war.

A Champion Sailor

What makes the Portuguese man-of-war a champion sailor? First, it can actually trim, or adjust, its balloonlike sail just as a human sailor would. When the wind blows, the animal sets to work like the crew of an old galleon. The man-of-war pumps and trims its sail to adjust it to the wind. With its streaming tentacles acting as a stabilizing sea anchor, the Portuguese man-of-war moves off with the breeze. The man-of-war uses its sailing skills to explore every ocean in the world. Because of prevailing winds in the Atlantic and Pacific oceans, the animals sail mainly towards coastal waters, where they find rich supplies of food.

The other finalist in our sailing competition would be the *velella*, a smaller relative of the Portuguese man-of-war. It has a fixed "sail" that is set either to the left or right of its body. The velella travels by the power of the wind, but it can't trim its sail as can the man-of-war. So the industrious Portugese man-of-war would have no difficulty in sailing away with the gold medal.

Rowing

Ducks were disqualified in the sailing contest and they would have to be banned from another Animalympic event—the rowing competition. Ducks and some other water birds such as coots don't row, they paddle. When they are in a hurry, steamer ducks beat their way across the water surface using their wings and feet like the paddle wheels of a steamboat. Our competitors actually row—they propel themselves through the water using their limbs as oars. By the time we reached the finals of this event there would only be two animal athletes to battle it out. One would be the turtle and the other would be a pond-dwelling insect called the *backswimmer*.

Stroke, Stroke

The backswimmer literally turns itself into a row boat. It lies on its back, which has a ridge resembling the keel of a boat, and sculls about. Air is trapped in rows of waterproof hairs at the sides of the backswimmer's plump abdomen and beneath its wings. This air enables the backswimmer to breath underwater for long periods of time and provides a lot of **buoyancy**. The

The water boatman rows just under the water's surface—upside down!

The matamata, a freshwater turtle from South America, is known for its strangely shaped head and neck.

backswimmer floats up to the water surface, seeming to hang underneath the water by its four front legs. The two rear legs, which are fringed with hair, form efficient oars. The backswimmer rows just under the surface, using its rear legs for power and its forelegs to cling to vegetation and capture prey. When it emerges from the water, either to climb onto a plant or to fly away, it bobs up stern (rear) first. Most species survive the winter as adults and may sometimes be seen rowing beneath the ice!

The backswimmer is a fierce predator. It mainly preys on other insects that swim on the surface of the water or fall into the pond. The backswimmer can inflict a powerful sting that can kill bigger water animals, including fish. It sometimes does a lot of damage in fishponds. The backswimmer is also known, appropriately, as the "water bee."

Water boatmen, which resemble backswimmers, are also good rowers. They feed on algae and spend a lot of time underwater, resting quietly and clinging to plants on the bottom of a pond or stream. Air trapped beneath the water boatman's wings makes the insect so buoyant that, like the backswimmer, it would float to the water's surface if it let go of its hold.

Paddles and Oars

Turtles, along with tortoises and terrapins, are members of the group of reptiles called *chelonians*. The chelonian's distinctive characteristic is its shell. Chelonians existed long before the age of the dinosaurs. Turtles and terrapins are aquatic—some live in fresh water, others live in the ocean—while tortoises live on land.

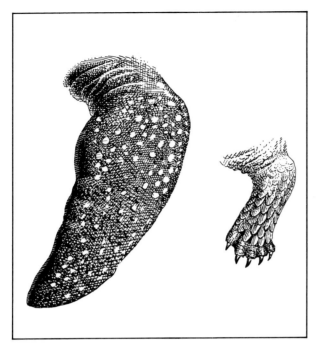

There are about 250 different species of turtles. The giant marine leatherback turtle can tip the scales at 1,500 pounds (675 kg) and perhaps even one ton. The little *bog turtle* is only 4 inches (10 cm) long. Some, such as *snapping turtles*, are known for their bad tempers and inclination to bite. Others, such as *musk turtles* of northern Central America, are famous for emitting a nasty smell from glands in their groin. The strange *matamata*, a South American freshwater species, is known for its rough, ridged shell and strange bumps, lumps, and flaps on its head and neck.

Turtles row through the water with their feet. In freshwater turtles, each clawed toe is distinct and is connected to the others by a webbing of skin. Marine turtles have a foot without distinct toes. The foot looks more like a flipper or an oar.

Above: The forelimb of a marine turtle (left) and that of a freshwater species (right). *Below:* A leatherback turtle digs a pit for her eggs.

A marine turtle rows to a gold medal.

Marine turtles normally row along at about 3.5 miles per hour (6 kph). But they are capable, if in danger, of spurts of up to 21 miles per hour (35 kph). Marine turtles also row great distances. A migrating Atlantic *green turtle* is on record as having swum 1,170 miles (1,950 km) in 270 days.

Marine turtles live all of their lives at sea, except during the vital and brief egg-laying season. Turtles must lay their eggs on land. To do so, the female laboriously hauls herself up onto a beach, usually at night, and buries her eggs in the sand or under vegetation. The eggs lie there untended and **incubate** in the warmth of the sun. Turtle eggs are at risk from predators such as wild pigs or even hungry humans. Adult turtles and tortoises have also been killed by people who seek the animals' shells and fresh meat. Tourism, building developments, and other human intrusions also gravely threaten the traditional breeding beaches of many species.

Unlike tortoises, which are **herbivores**, marine turtles eat both meat and vegetation. Some freshwater turtles are carnivorous, feeding on fish and other small animals such as snails and prawns. One species, the *alligator snapping turtle*, feeds on fish that it attracts to its gaping beak by wiggling a wormlike attachment on its tongue as bait.

Like other reptiles, turtles breathe air. But the turtle's solid shell prevents much chest movement. How then do turtles pass air in and out of their lungs? Movements of the head and legs, together with a pumping movement of the throat, help force air into the turtle's lungs. Some small species can also draw oxygen directly from the water into their skin.

While they rarely attain great speeds, turtles are the fastest swimmers of all the *four-legged* animals. In the Animalympic rowing competition, the marine turtle would easily take the gold medal.

Gymnastics

The gymnastic competition in our Animalympics would be totally dominated by the primates—the order of mammals that includes lemurs, bush babies, monkeys, apes, and humans. There would be talented entrants from all over the world. A colorful and ever-active bunch of marmosets and tamarins would come from South America. Graceful lemurs would arrive from Madagascar. There would be handsome colobus monkeys and quaint tarsiers from Africa, a golden monkey with a blue face from China, noisy rhesus monkeys from India, and crab-eating macaques from the Far East.

The event would test agility and grace both on the ground and on the natural horizontal bars, trapezes, and vaulting horses that make up the the jungle. *Barbary apes* of Gibraltar and *baboons* of Africa and Saudi Arabia spend most of their time on the ground and might not make it beyond the first heat. The *gorilla* is not quite graceful enough and would probably be eliminated in the semifinals. Eventually, the lineup for the finals would include a number of lemurs, some South American monkeys, a chimpanzee, and the gibbons from the forests of the Far East. The winner would most likely be a tree-dwelling specialist.

Versatility and Grace

The *chimpanzee* is a talented gymnast. It displays great muscular power and nimbleness. On the ground, it can shuffle, roll, somersault, stamp, rock from one leg to

another, run on all fours in a rather ungainly manner called "knuckle-walking," and walk

The emperor tamarin, with its elaborate mustache, is one of the best monkey gymnasts.

30

A baby chimpanzee hitches a ride on its mother's back. The chimp is a versatile gymnast.

on its hind legs like a tipsy sailor. Off the ground, it can climb and swing effortlessly by one or both hands or feet. Like other primates, the chimp has an opposable thumb, which can move freely and press against the palm of the hand. This type of thumb enables primates to grasp things firmly and it gives them considerable dexterity. No other animal, except a human, is a more versatile user of tools than the chimpanzee. Chimps use sticks and stems to probe ant and termite holes for food. They employ stones and sticks to break open fruit. They also throw sticks and rocks, turn leaves into flyswatters, and chew bark

and vegetation into balls that they use as sponges. Although it is clever, the chimpanzee isn't as elegant and delicate in its movements as some of the other competitors. In the Animalympic gymnastic event, as in the human Olympics, it's not just what you do, but how you do it.

Another gymnastic finalist would be the graceful *gibbon*. Nine species of gibbons live in the jungles of southeast Asia. They specialize in trapeze work among the trees and they move with incredible skill. The gibbon has long, muscular arms and legs, highly flexible shoulders, and no tail. The gibbon spends two hours per day traveling through the jungle. It moves from branch to branch at high speed by swinging with one arm and then the other. This kind of locomotion is known as *brachiation*. As it swings hand over hand through the jungle, the gibbon demonstrates the most fluid movement of any tree-dwelling creature. The gibbon is also more able than any other ape to stand upright like a human.

On the move or when sitting still, the gibbon provides us with an additional delightful display—its singing. Where chimps grunt, hoot, and shriek, gibbons make sounds of great beauty and complexity. One of the most memorable experiences of a trip to the Far Eastern jungle is to hear the calls of the gibbons, particularly in the early morning. The songs, often performed as duets, carry for great distances. Some types of gibbons have developed inflatable throat sacs that **resonate** and increase the volume of the call. The male gibbon frequently sings to warn other gibbons that a certain patch of jungle is occupied. The female often sings to warn other females away from her mate. Gibbons are strongly territorial. Each gibbon family proudly possesses one area of forest—and wants there to be no doubt about it!

Acrobats of the Treetops

The lemur would also qualify for the gymnastic finals. There are about 23 species of lemurs alive today and all inhabit the forests of the island of Madagascar, off the coast of eastern Africa. When humans first arrived on Madagascar about 2,000 years ago, there were many more kinds of lemurs living there, including a giant one, as big as an orangutan. As in so many other cases, humans had a massive impact. People interfered with the lemur's environment and hunted the animals. At least 15 species soon became extinct. Now, only smaller species

exist. Their weights vary from a few ounces up to 22 pounds (10 kg). Measuring only 10 to 12 inches (25 to 30 cm) from the top of its head to the end of its tail, the *mouse lemur* is the smallest of all primates. The *hairy-eared mouse lemur* was once thought to be the rarest of all primates, but this title may now go to a new lemur, *Apalemur aureus*, first discovered in June 1987. Eating habits vary from species to species. Some lemurs eat bamboo shoots, and others prefer to gather nectar. Still other lemurs, such as the highly endangered, **nocturnal** *aye-aye*, seek out fruit and insect grubs. Most lemurs are wonderful at leaping among the forest trees. Some, such as the aptly named *sportive lemur*, are

The beautiful songs of the gibbons carry through the jungles of the Far East.

Spider monkeys swing through the trees with one arm and then the other.

adept at jumping from one tree trunk to another with their bodies held in a vertical position. *Ring-tailed lemurs* are very agile on the ground, where, unlike other lemur species, they spend most of their time. The rare *indri* is a lemur with a unique way of hopping along with its arms outstretched, which makes it look like a little, furry ballet dancer!

However, the best of all the primate gymnasts are the South American monkeys. They can be divided into two groups. The first group is composed of the tiny *marmosets* and *tamarins*, which have curved claws on most of their toes and fingers that enable them to climb quickly up the trunks of trees.

The second group contains the bigger monkeys such as *capuchins, spider monkeys,* and *woolly monkeys.* The great advantage that this latter group possesses is the prehensile, or grasping, tail. The tail acts like a fifth limb. It can hold onto a branch and carry all the weight of the monkey. This special type of tail—seen in no other primate—allows these monkeys of the Western Hemisphere to perform the widest possible repertoire of aerial movements.

Our gold medalist would most likely be one of these South American monkeys. After lengthy deliberation, the judges would finally give the medal to the graceful spider monkey—the champion acrobat of the treetops.

Weightlifting

The great apes—the chimpanzees, orangutans, and gorillas—make human weightlifters look puny by comparison. The smallest of the three, the chimp, is much stronger than an adult man, and the orangutan and gorilla are stronger still. The gorilla might win its heat in our weightlifting event but would probably be beaten in the semifinals by one of the biggest and one of the smallest contestants.

The elephant's trunk proves very handy when it's time for a quick drink of water or a bath.

The Versatile Elephant

The runner-up in the weightlifting event would be the *elephant*, the largest living land mammal, which can measure up to 13 feet (4 m) tall at the shoulder and can weigh 5 to 10 tons. Apart from humans, elephants fear no animal on earth. Long ago there were over 350 species of elephants on earth. These included a dwarf elephant that lived on the island of Crete and was only 3.3 feet (1 m) high as well as a 16.5-foot (5-m) tall giant, whose fossil remains were found in the English county of Kent. Elephants once inhabited not only countries with warm climates, but also colder northern regions, even the polar zones. Now only two kinds of elephants survive—the African and the Asiatic, or Indian, elephants.

Elephants can lift great weights by using their trunks and tusks. They can uproot trees and break off branches as thick as a man's thigh. For this reason, they have been domesticated by humans for at least 5,500 years. They are still used for moving timber and carrying heavy loads in India and parts of Asia where there are no roads and tractors and trucks cannot operate. Although nowadays only the Asiatic elephant is trained for work in this way, in bygone times, the African species was similarly employed. Elephants were enlisted by the armies of Rome and Carthage to terrify the enemy, charge through enemy ranks, scatter soldiers,

The elephant can uproot trees with its powerful trunk.

and crush them underfoot. The great Carthaginian general, Hannibal, crossed the Alps from France to invade Italy in 218 B.C. with a squad of 37 elephants. Historians still argue as to whether these were African or Indian elephants. In Hannibal's day, African elephants still lived in the wild in North Africa where Carthage was situated. Evidence provided by coins of the period does not settle the argument. Carthaginian coins minted in 220 B.C., two years before the expedition, bear the images of African elephants. Italian coins of 217 B.C. show those of the Indian species. If any of Hannibal's elephants died on the long march, maybe their bones are still buried somewhere in the French or Italian mountain passes. They could be **excavated** and their identification would solve the puzzle once and for all.

Big animals like elephants require plenty of food to keep them going. An adult elephant in the wild will eat 440 to 660 pounds (200 to 300 kg) of vegetable food and will drink around 40 gallons (152 liters) of water each day. The trunk of the elephant is a powerful, multipurpose tool. It is used for sniffing (an elephant's sense of smell is very acute); for sucking up water, which the elephant then squirts into its mouth; for blowing cool dust over the body; and for delicately touching other elephants in gestures of friendship and love. The trunk can also make a range of noises, from a deafening trumpet sound to a hollow boom produced when the trunk

is thumped against the ground. The trunk is also used to beat, pull, push, and break things.

Elephants usually walk at between 2 and 3 miles per hour (3 and 5 kph). When they charge, they can reach speeds of around 19 miles per hour (32 kph). They only use four teeth at any one time. As the four molar teeth at the front of the elephant's mouth wear down, they fall out and are replaced by new ones that move forward from the back. Throughout its life an elephant can call on a total of 24 molars. If the teeth are all used up, an elephant in the wild will starve to death. Elephants can live to a ripe old age of 70 years and perhaps more. They have the longest pregnancy period of any mammal—21 to 23 months. Females have two breasts, situated between their front legs, which are used for giving milk to their young. The elephant's closest living relative is the *hyrax*, a furry little animal without a trunk that weighs only 2 to 11 pounds (1 to 5 kg). The hyrax looks like a large guinea pig. It is found in Africa and parts of the Middle East.

Although elephants are wonderful lifters and phenomenally strong, they can't equal what another finalist can do—lift something many times its own body weight. In the Animalympics, the competitor who can do this couldn't even be seen through binoculars by the audience in the stands of the stadium. It is the *ant*.

Small but Mighty

Insects, for their size, are far stronger than any reptile or mammal. Dung beetles, grasshoppers, and fleas can all can push, pull, or lift objects far heavier than themselves. Among the strongest of all insects is the ant, which can carry objects 50 times heavier than itself. The ant is one of the most widely distributed insects on this planet. Ants are found in abundance almost everywhere and they comprise a vast number of species. We are all familiar with the 1/5-inch (5-mm) black garden ant, which regularly enters houses to **forage** for sweet food. But there are far tinier ants, such as one from Sri Lanka that is a mere 1/30th of an inch (0.8 mm) in length. There are also giant ants in Africa, Australia, and South America that can measure up to 2 inches (5 cm) in length.

Ants, like many bees, are social animals. They live in colonies that consist of one or several fertile female **queens** and a large number—often thousands—of sterile females

An ant drags a dead cockroach that is many times its own size.

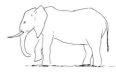

or "workers." The worker ants are much smaller than the queens and have no wings. Males are winged and emerge from the nest only when the ants swarm. During this flight, the male ants mate with the queen and then quickly die.

Different species of ants display different behavior. Some, such as the *fire ant* of South, Central, and southern North America have powerful stingers on the tip of their abdomens. The black *bulldog ant* of Australia both stings and bites when attacking. The nomadic *army ants* of the Western Hemisphere and the *driver ants* of Africa periodically go on great marches, killing and eating any creature that gets in their way. Columns of these ants—over a mile long, half a mile wide, and numbering many millions of insects—are sometimes seen in the tropics. Sometimes the column splits in two to surround a likely victim and it may devour a large animal such as a tethered goat or horse. Other ants are not carnivores, but are herbivores that live in intricate "towns" that they have constructed. Some ants nest in the ground or in wood, excavating systems of tunnels and chambers. Others build nests of "paper" made from leaves or chewed wood pulp.

Gardeners and Farmers

While some ants feed on seeds or raid people's pantries for sugary foods, others are gardeners that grow fungus on **compost** beds in their underground cities. The compost is made from fermenting bits of leaves that the ants cut from trees near the nest and carry home. *Leaf-cutting ants* of this type often walk along with a portion of a leaf—weighing much more than themselves—carried above their heads like a banner. The fungus is carefully tended by the worker ants and each queen carries a piece of the fungus in her throat when she goes off to set up a new nest.

Some ants are dairy farmers that keep "herds" of **aphids** in their nests. The ants "milk" these insects, which, after sucking the juices of plants, secrete a sweet liquid called honeydew. *Honey ants* gather sweet food from insects and plants. Some of the worker honey ants act as living honeypots. They store the sweet liquid in their stomachs until their abdomens are so swollen that they cannot move. When other members of the ant colony are hungry, they tap on the **antennae** of the "honeypots." The honeypots then obligingly vomit up some of the food inside them!

There are also ants that are *slave-makers*. They raid the nests of other ants, kill the workers, and kidnap the other ants' larvae, which in due time emerge as workers in the raiders' nests.

Leaf-cutting ants on the march. The ants will grow fungus from bits of the fermented leaves.

Despite differences in size, diet, and behavior, all ants are powerful weightlifters. Not even the mighty elephant can compete with the ant's ability to lift objects many times heavier than itself. Pound for pound, the ant is the champion lifter of the animal kingdom and is surely the Animalympic weightlifting gold medalist.

The Marathon

Many animal athletes perform baffling feats of endurance and skill, but the Animalympic marathon contestants might be the most intriguing of them all. The marathon, of course, is a long-distance race. In our marathon, contestants might travel by land, air, or water. The varied and colorful band of competitors, coming from almost all families within the animal kingdom, go on regular long-distance journeys for all sorts of reasons. They go in search of food, they go to breeding grounds, and they go to spend the winter in the sun.

An Insect Invasion

One of the most beautiful and delicate of the contestants would be the *monarch butterfly*, greatest of all insect marathon specialists. A large, black and orange butterfly with white spots on its wings and body, the monarch is native to North America. It roosts in trees with thousands of its fellow butterflies. It is astonishing to come across a "butterfly tree" during the winter in California, Florida, or Mexico. The butterflies resemble autumn leaves as they perch in the trees (the monarchs

The spectacular monarch butterfly undertakes a marathon flight each spring.

The Norwegian lemming might not make it to the finish line on its marathon journey.

use the same ones every year). When warm weather arrives at the end of March, the monarchs fly north, sometimes in great swarms up to 2 miles (3 km) long and hundreds of feet wide. Within two months, they reach Canada and Hudson Bay. In September, a new generation of monarchs flies straight back to the homes and favorite trees of its parents—over 2,000 miles (3,200 km) away.

Very long journeys are also made by painted lady butterflies, cabbage white butterflies, and some moths, dragonflies, and ladybugs. The *locust* is a long-distance athlete that can eat its own weight in food every day. A locust swarm can destroy millions of dollars worth of crops as it travels. A swarm may be so thick that it blots out the sunlight. A locust may fly 2,000 miles (3,200 km) while migrating.

The Mystery of Long-Distance Travel

How do insects navigate over such great distances? The answer is not fully known. Some insects have mysterious internal clocks and compasses that help them make their flight calculations. Many insects have sophisticated compound eyes that act like sun compasses. The compound eye works like an array of computer screens connected to a central computer. As the insect travels, each screen of its eye registers the position of the sun in the sky and the animal is then able to calculate its path through the air. Insects might also use their sense of smell to navigate. Butterflies have a better sense of smell than most animals. The butterfly's antennae each carry tens of thousands of "sniffing" nerve cells that help the insect locate plants and other butterflies as it travels.

Amazing Journeys by Land, Sea, and Air

The *Norwegian lemming* would be eliminated in our marathon semifinals. This mouselike rodent is famous purely for its mass migrations that sometimes end in death. Every few years, thousands and thousands of lemmings migrate across the tundra of Scandinavia with more and more lemmings

A champion long-distance flier, an Arctic tern rides the wind.

joining the throng as they go. Eventually, a kind of mass panic sets in and the lemmings dash heedlessly into rivers, over cliffs, and sometimes into the sea. Although lemmings are good swimmers, they drown in large numbers.

The great *whalebone*, or *baleen*, whales are the champion mammal marathon contestants. They swim many thousands of miles to find breeding grounds and food. As they go, some whales sing beautiful songs.

The *turtle*, another long-distance competitor, also makes marathon marine journeys. Green turtles may migrate thousands of miles from the Brazilian coast to nest on Ascension Island in the South Atlantic Ocean. Some scientists have suggested that turtles navigate partly by using the rumblings of underwater volcanos as sound beacons. But turtles are also great sniffers in water. In the 1920s, a snapping turtle attached to a long line was used by its Native American handler to find the corpses of murder victims submerged in a lake.

The bird finalists would include the *sooty albatross*, which each year flies around the globe, covering 228 miles (380 km) a day for some 80 days. The *Arctic tern* would also qualify. One Arctic tern is on record as migrating 13,440 miles (22,400 km) from the White Sea in the northeast Soviet Union to Australia in just over 10 months! A surprise flying champion is the minute *rufous hummingbird*, which journeys 2,000 miles (3,200 km) each autumn from Alaska to Mexico and returns in the spring.

No one knows for sure how birds are able to navigate with accuracy over such great distances. Certainly, birds follow landmarks such as rivers and mountain ranges when they migrate. But scientists also believe that birds may be guided by the earth's magnetic field, the angle of the sun, and the position of stars and planets in the sky.

The Epic Journey of the Eel

Some well-known fish, including tuna, cod, and herring, would be eliminated in the quarterfinals of the Animalympic marathon contest. One fish that would make it to the finals, however, would be the *eel*. The eel's epic journeys are very strange affairs. American and European eels are born in the Sargasso Sea, the seaweed-clogged part of the Atlantic Ocean between the Azores Islands and the West Indies. The young eels at once set off to float and swim—some to Europe and some to America—a distance of up to 3,000 miles (5,000 km). After three years they arrive and swim inland along rivers and into ponds and lakes. They even reach alpine streams at altitudes of almost 10,000 feet (3,000 m). The eels stay inland for up to nine years and then, as mature adults, make their way back to the rivers and retrace their path to the Sargasso Sea where they breed and then die. They are helped along on the return journey, which takes about seven months, by deep underwater currents. During their journey, they do not feed, but rely on their stores of body fat.

No one quite understands the uncanny accuracy of an eel's navigational abilities, particularly in deep, dark water. Perhaps it gets clues from the direction of water currents. Certainly, it has an amazing sense of smell—almost as good as the butterfly's. A sense of smell can be just as important under water as it is on land. Under water a good nose is more useful than eyes. Perhaps the eel can pick up distinctive scents in the water at its journey's end.

With so many animal marathoners it would be difficult to determine the long-distance champion. After lengthy deliberation the judges would finally make their decision. For its ability to navigate with uncanny precision over thousands of miles, through numerous seas and waterways, in a journey that might take several years, the eel would be named our Animalympic marathon gold medalist.

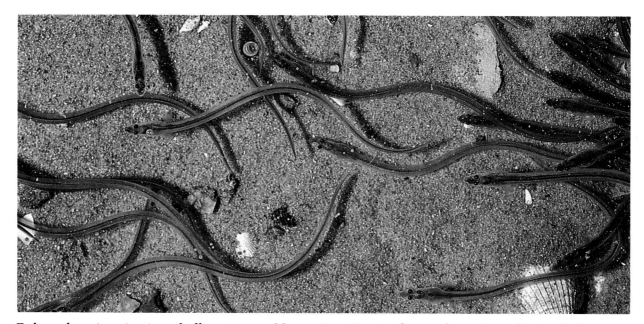

Baby eels swimming in a shallow stream. No one is quite sure how eels navigate during their epic underwater journey.

The Decathlon

And now the final event in our Animalympiad—the decathlon, the contest for brilliant all-arounders that will decide who is to be crowned the Bruce Jenner of the animal kingdom. All animal species are expert in at least one, and often more than one, aspect of athletics. They keep themselves fit—they have to, for their survival depends on it. An overweight lion would not be able to catch its prey. A rabbit that dozed lazily all day in the sunlit grass of a meadow would quickly fall prey to the fox or hunter. Hummingbirds and shrews must work long hours to gather all the food they need to stay alive, and a colobus monkey that is anything but a tiptop gymnast will quickly attract the attention of a hungry eagle or chimpanzee.

Many creatures are *specialist* athletes—world-class performers in one particular event. The swift can stay on the wing month after month. Cheetahs are sprinters, and the pronghorn antelope of the United States is the master of fast, long-distance running. For feats of strength we think of the elephant, the gorilla, and the great whales, as well

The chimpanzee is a talented all-arounder, but is it good enough to win the decathlon?

The knuckle-walking chimpanzee

as insects such as ants and dung beetles. But the decathlon is for all-arounders—superathletes. Which animal species best fits the bill?

In the finals of our decathlon there would be a wide variety of contestants. The dolphin is a champion swimmer, diver, and jumper, but obviously would not do too well in the dry land portion of the competition. The great northern diver is a good flier and a superb diver that can reach depths of 165 feet (50 m) and possibly 230 feet (70 m) in water. But it wouldn't be in contention for the running, jumping, or weightlifting events. And although the flea could thrill the crowd with its jumping abilities, its swimming and running skills are abysmal.

One finalist, the chimpanzee, is a strong weightlifter, a most accomplished gymnast, and quite a good jumper. It is quick, but not as fast as a leopard or a lion. Chimps, unlike most animal athletes, are also quite good at throwing things—an important skill for

human decathlon contestants. Although not as skilled as a human javelin or discus thrower, the chimp can hurl rocks and sticks weighing several pounds with reasonable accuracy. Just as people once went hunting with throwing sticks or boomerangs, chimpanzees have been seen to throw sticks at ferocious wild pigs with accuracy from a distance of over 16 feet (5 m). When the surprised pigs run off, the chimps then dash in to snatch up the piglets.

But the chimpanzee isn't fond of water (except to drink) and is certainly not much of a swimmer. It would only be a runner-up in the decathlon.

The Striped Marvel

There is one animal athlete that is so strong, swift, and agile that it stands out above all others as the all-around champion. It is the largest member of the cat family— the *tiger*. Usually a loner, the tiger is one of the most accomplished as well as one of the most beautiful animals on earth. And look at its athletic prowess. It is a fast runner—at full gallop it will clear 13 feet (4 m) in one bound. A great hunter, the tiger stalks its victim silently, crouches and waits in ambush, and then sprints in to make the kill. The tiger walks gracefully, with both limbs on one side of its body moving forward together. A tiger may walk 12 to 30 miles (20 to 50 km) in a day, and a Siberian tiger was once tracked covering 600 miles (1,000 km) in 22 days.

Although they are not regular climbers, tigers do climb very effectively. They have gone up trees to seize people who have shinnied up into what they thought was a safe refuge. They have also been seen climbing effortlessly over 13-foot (4-m) wire fences in safari parks. As long-jumpers, tigers have certainly achieved 23-foot (7-m) and perhaps even 33-foot (10-m) leaps. Manchurian tigers

sometimes ambush wild pigs (their main diet in some areas) by lying concealed on the edge of a cliff and then jumping down on their prey to deliver a deadly neck bite.

The tiger also swims very well. Although swimming is not tested in the human decathlon, it is a very important skill for an animal athlete. Among the wild cats, only the jaguar and the fishing cat adore water more than the tiger. Tigers are often found near water and on hot days they cool off in pools or streams. They can easily swim 3 miles (5 km), and have been known to paddle out to attack people in boats. In the Sundarbans, the great mangrove swamp area of the Ganges delta in India, tiger attacks are still a problem. A tiger has even been seen in the middle of a

broad river engaged in a tug-of-war contest with a crocodile over a sambar deer carcass.

Tigers are also immensely strong. They have been known to take on formidable heavyweight adversaries, including bears. Tigers do not just attack the small sloth bear of eastern India and Sri Lanka, they also take on the Himalayan black and Siberian brown bears, which can weigh up to 605 pounds (275 kg)—as much as a fully grown male tiger.

Tigers also sometimes kill wolves, leopards, young elephants, and buffalo, employing their enormously powerful bite to overcome their prey. Tigers rarely attack adult elephants, but it has happened. In one case, two tigers battled with a big tusker (male elephant) for

The powerful tiger excels in a number of athletic events.

An accomplished swimmer, the tiger is at home in water as well as on land.

three hours before they finally overcame it. It is possible that tigers trick their prey by imitating them when they are out hunting. Some people believe that the tiger's so-called pook noise is an imitation of the sambar's call, while others think that the sound is simply used for communication between tigers. It has also been suggested that the Siberian tiger imitates the mating roar made by the male elk.

Having made a kill, the tiger often demonstrates its weightlifting talents. It may carry or drag a heavy carcass over a considerable distance. One tiger was seen tugging along a dead, 440-pound (200-kg) buffalo for more than a third of a mile (1/2 km).

The tiger is certainly the all-arounder, displaying a wider range of athletic ability than any other competitor. It would surely take the gold medal in our decathlon. As it mounted the victor's podium at the end of the Animalympics, the tiger would make a most handsome spectacle with which to close the games.

The Animalympiad CHAMPION

Glossary

accelerate To gain speed

antenna A sense organ on the head of an insect, used for smelling and touching

aphid A small insect that sucks the juices of plants

aquatic Growing or living in water

buoyancy The tendency of a body to float or rise when submerged in water

carnivore An animal that eats meat

cold-blooded Having a body temperature consistent with the temperature of the environment; unable to generate its own heat

compost Decaying vegetable matter

domesticated Tamed; adapted to living and breeding near humans

dorsal Situated on the back of an animal

evolve To change as a race or species

excavate To dig out and remove

forage To wander in search of food

gill An organ used for obtaining oxygen from water

herbivore An animal that eats only plants

hydraulics A branch of science that deals with liquid in motion

incubate To provide warmth that causes eggs to hatch

insulate To prevent the transfer of heat from one body to another

invertebrate An animal lacking a spinal column

jet propulsion Forward movement resulting from the rearward discharge of a jet of fluid

larva The early form of an animal that at birth or hatching is unlike its parent

mammal A warm-blooded animal with hair that feeds its young with milk

marsupial A member of the group of mammals that includes kangaroos, wombats, and opossums. Marsupials usually have a pouch on the abdomen of the female for carrying the young.

nocturnal Active at night

predator An animal that kills and eats other animals

primate A member of the group of mammals that includes humans, apes, monkeys, and lemurs

queen A fertile female bee, ant, or termite whose function is to lay eggs

resonate to vibrate in order to amplify and enrich sound

tentacle A long projection from an animal's body that helps the animal grasp or feel objects or prey

vertical Upright; perpendicular to the horizon

warm-blooded Having a constant body temperature regardless of the temperature of the surroundings; able to generate its own heat

Index

Acknowledgments

Illustrations and photographs are reproduced through the courtesy of Bruce Coleman Limited: pp. 6 (Erwin and Peggy Bauer), 7 (Fritz Prenzel), 10 (Kim Taylor), 12, 24 (Jen and Des Bartlett), 14 (Francisco Erizo), 15, 28 (R and M Borland), 26 (Dr. Eckart Pott), 30 (L. C. Marigo), 31, 43 (Helmut Albrecht), 32 (C.B. Frith), 40 (Gordon Langsbury), 45 (Hans Reinhard)/Oxford Scientific Film Stills: pp. 9, 13, 16, 18, 19, 20, 23, 27, 37, 39, 41/Planet Earth Pictures: pp. 24, 34/Premaphotos Wildlife: p. 36. Front cover: C. Allan Morgan. Other illustrations: David Quinn.

David Taylor is a veterinarian who works with wild animals around the world. From the Komodo dragon to the giant panda, from killer whales to gorillas, Taylor specializes in the problems that can beset the rare, the exotic, and the endangered.

His adventures have been recounted in his autobiographical series of *Zoovet* books and in the popular television series, "One by One," which has been shown in Great Britain, the United States, and many other countries. David Taylor has recently retraced Hannibal's epic journey across the Alps—with elephants—and has been involved in the rescue of two dolphins stranded in Egypt.